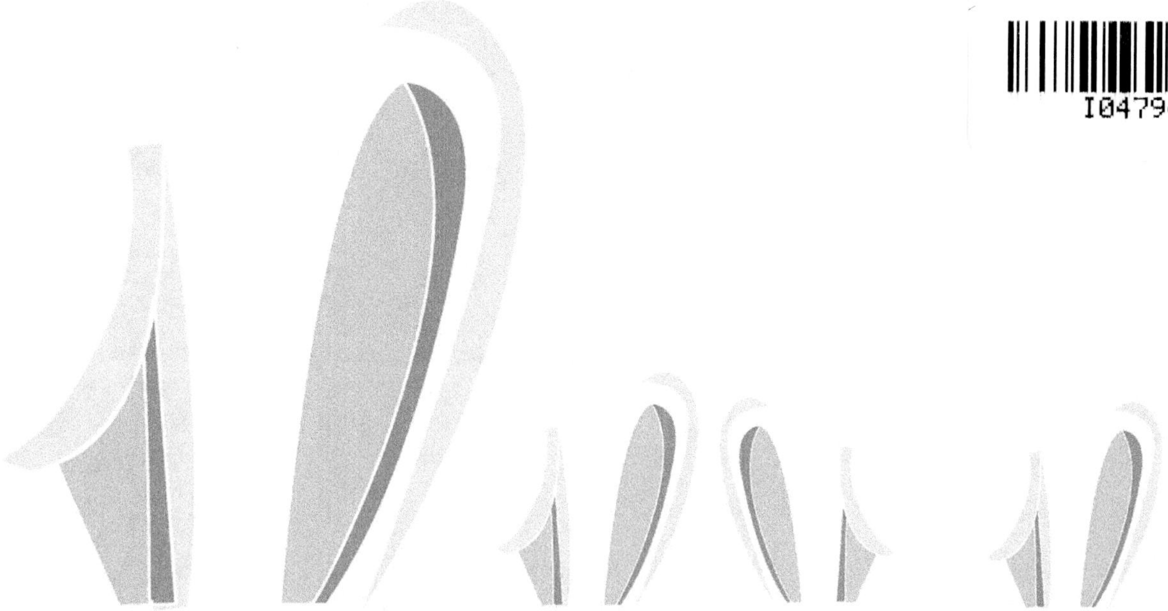

# This book belongs to

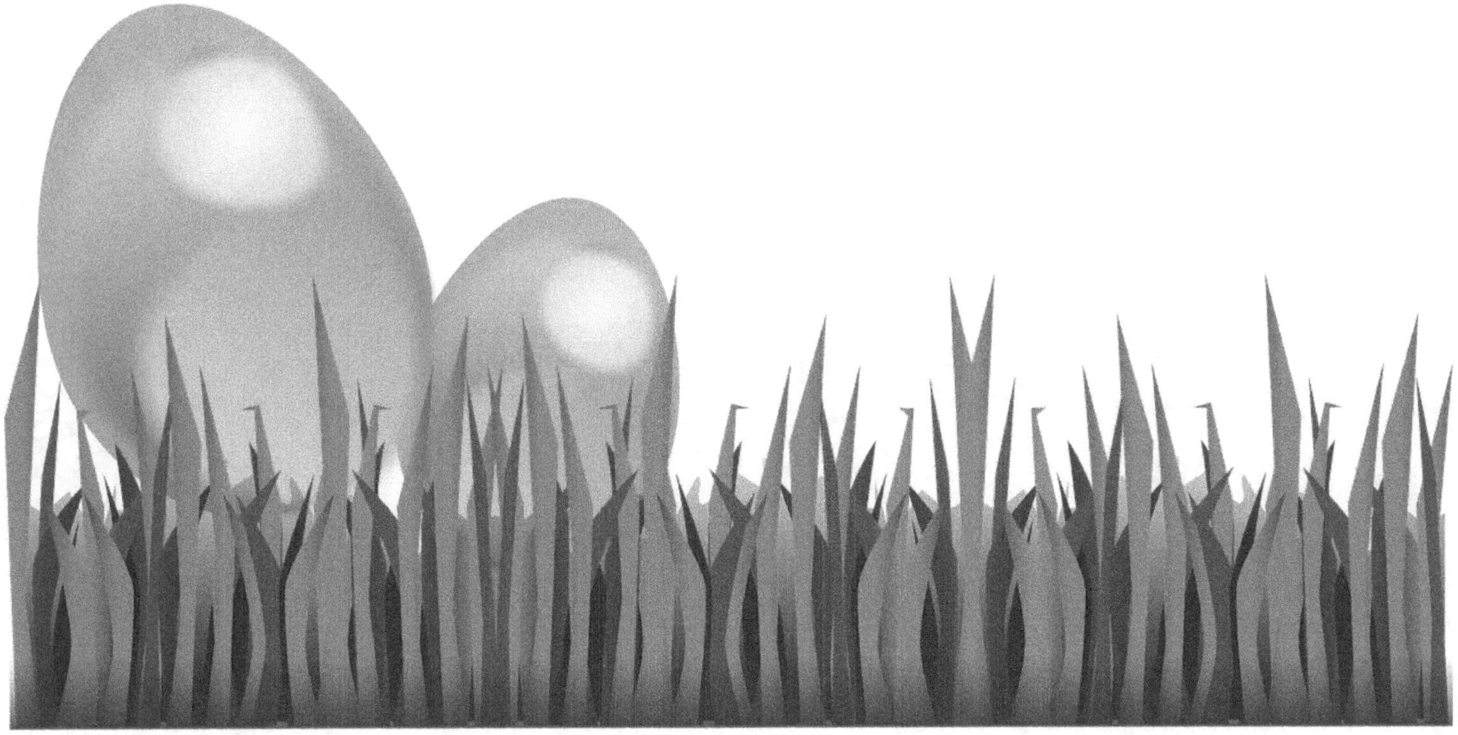

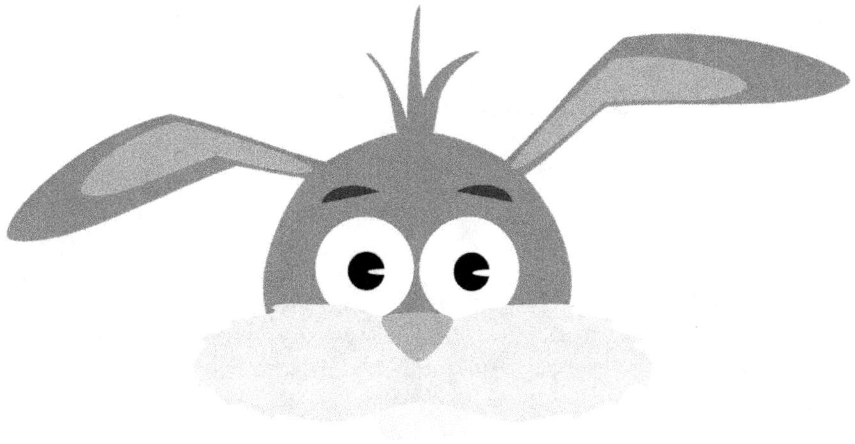

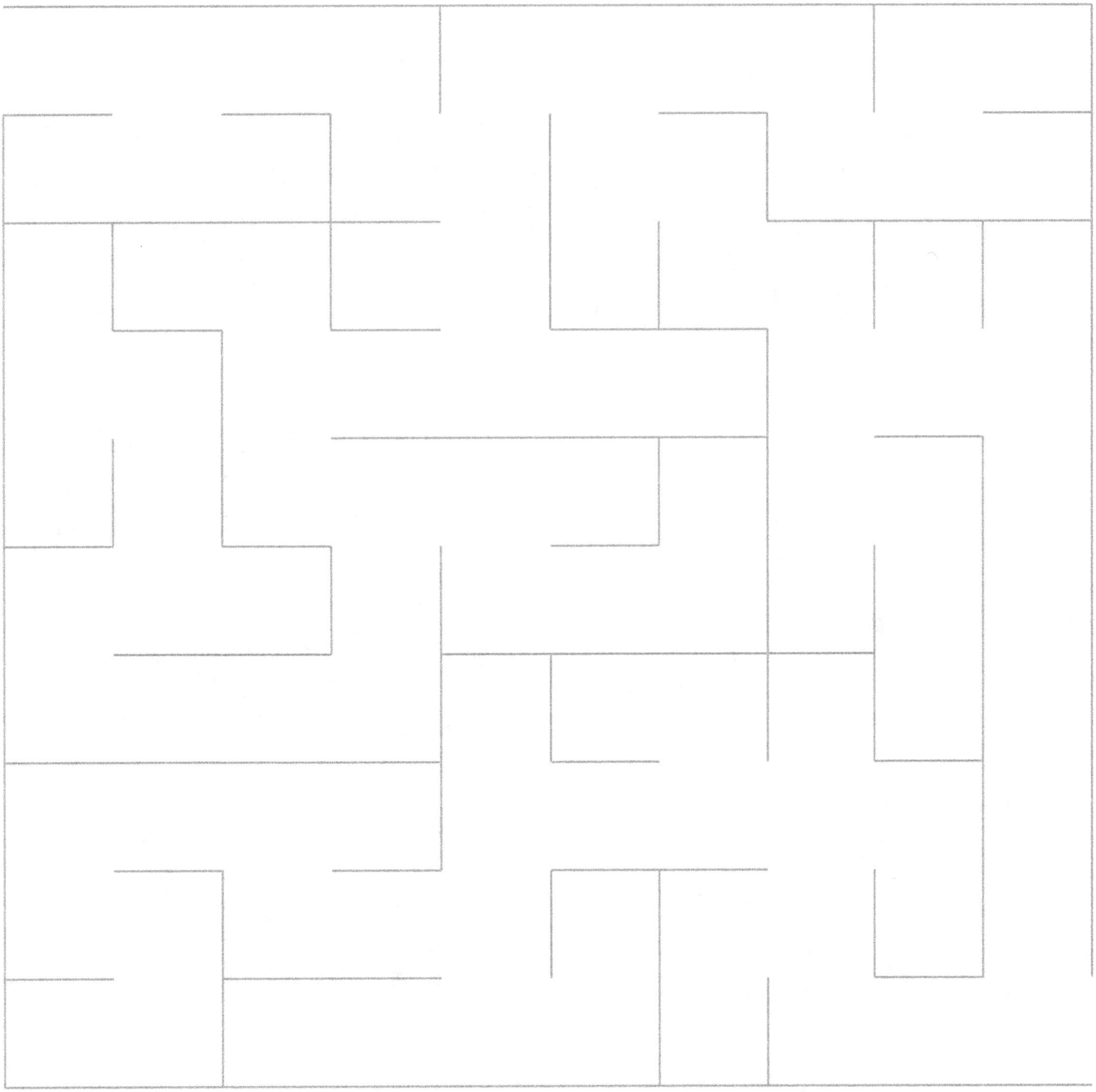

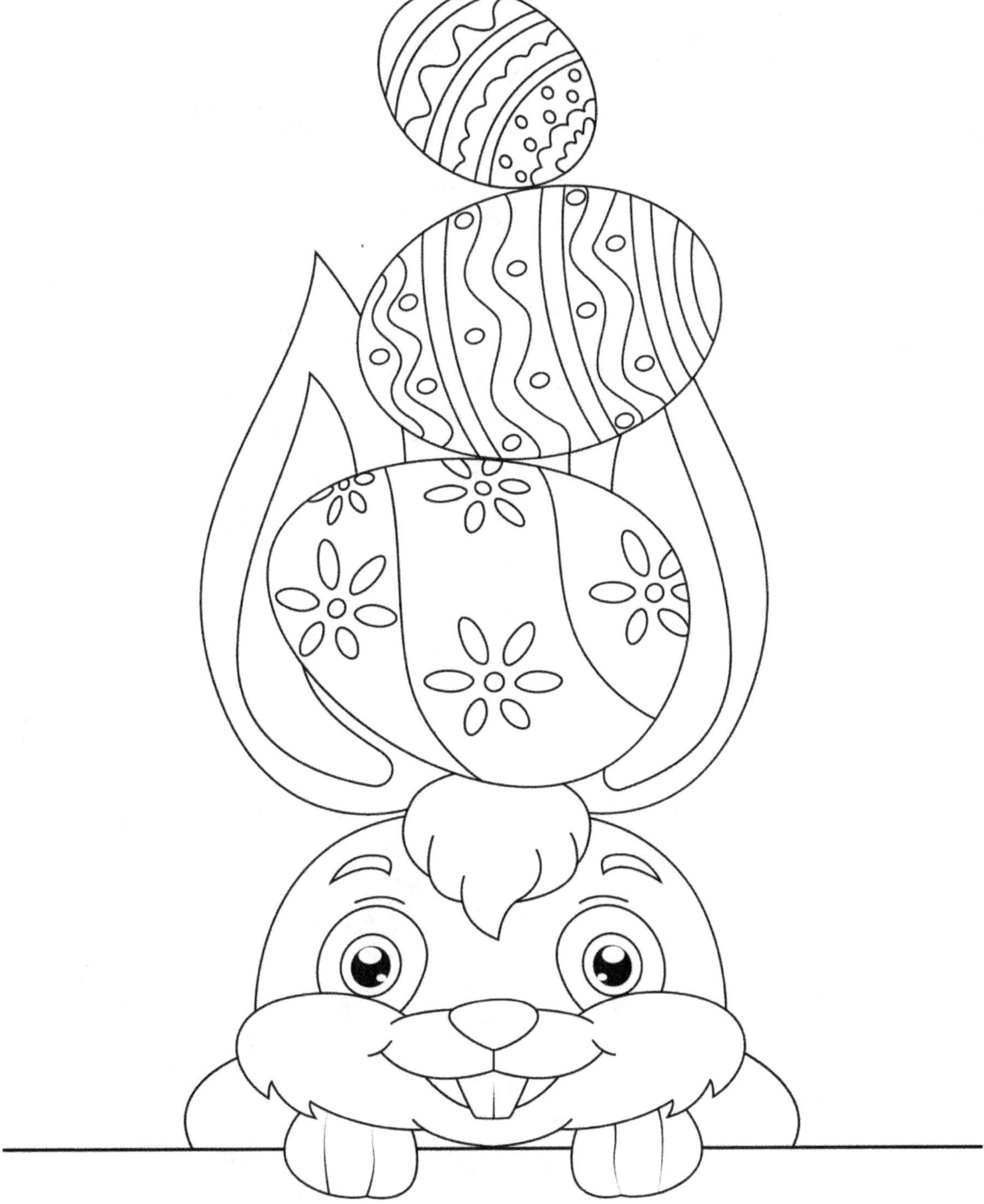

# Match the halves

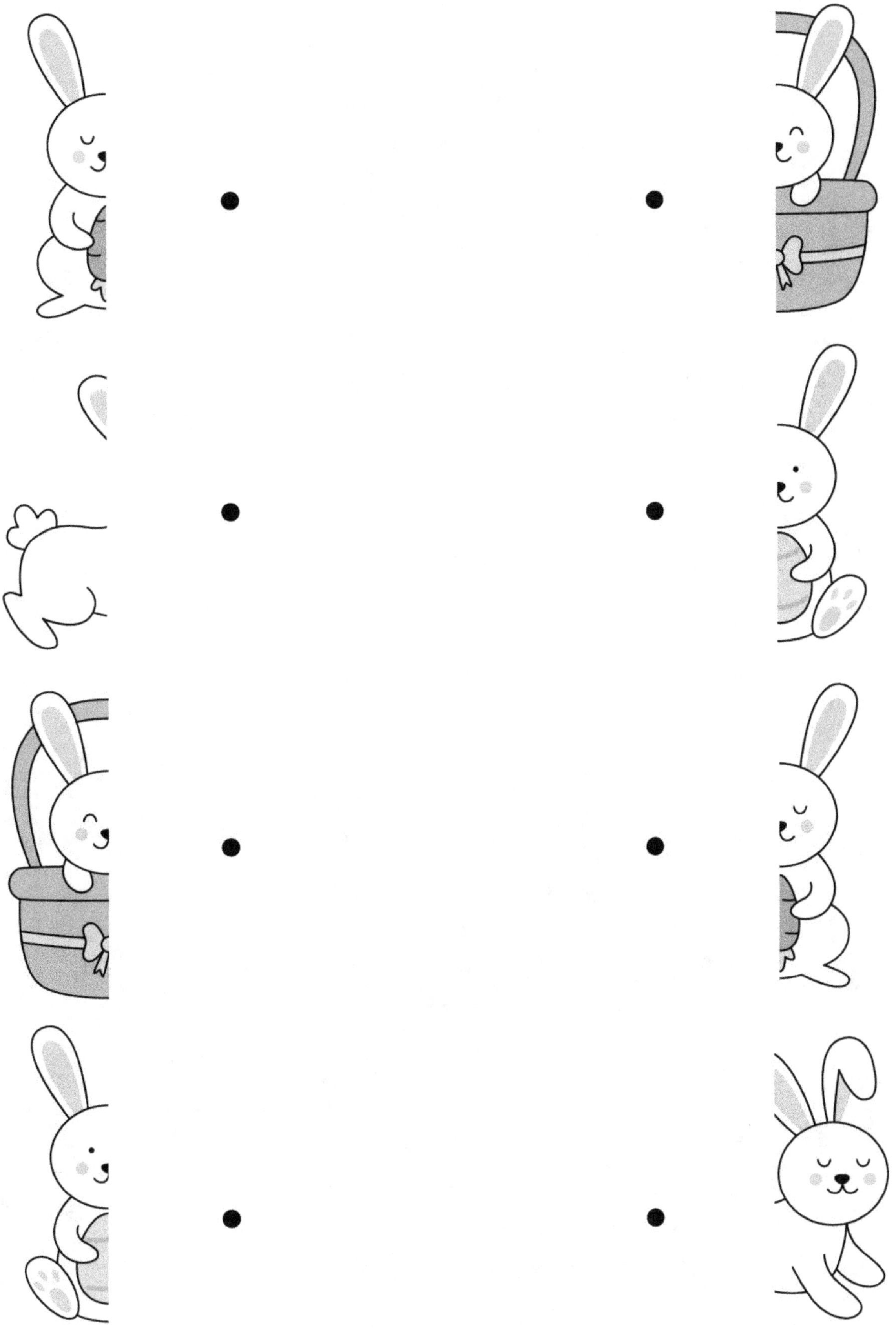

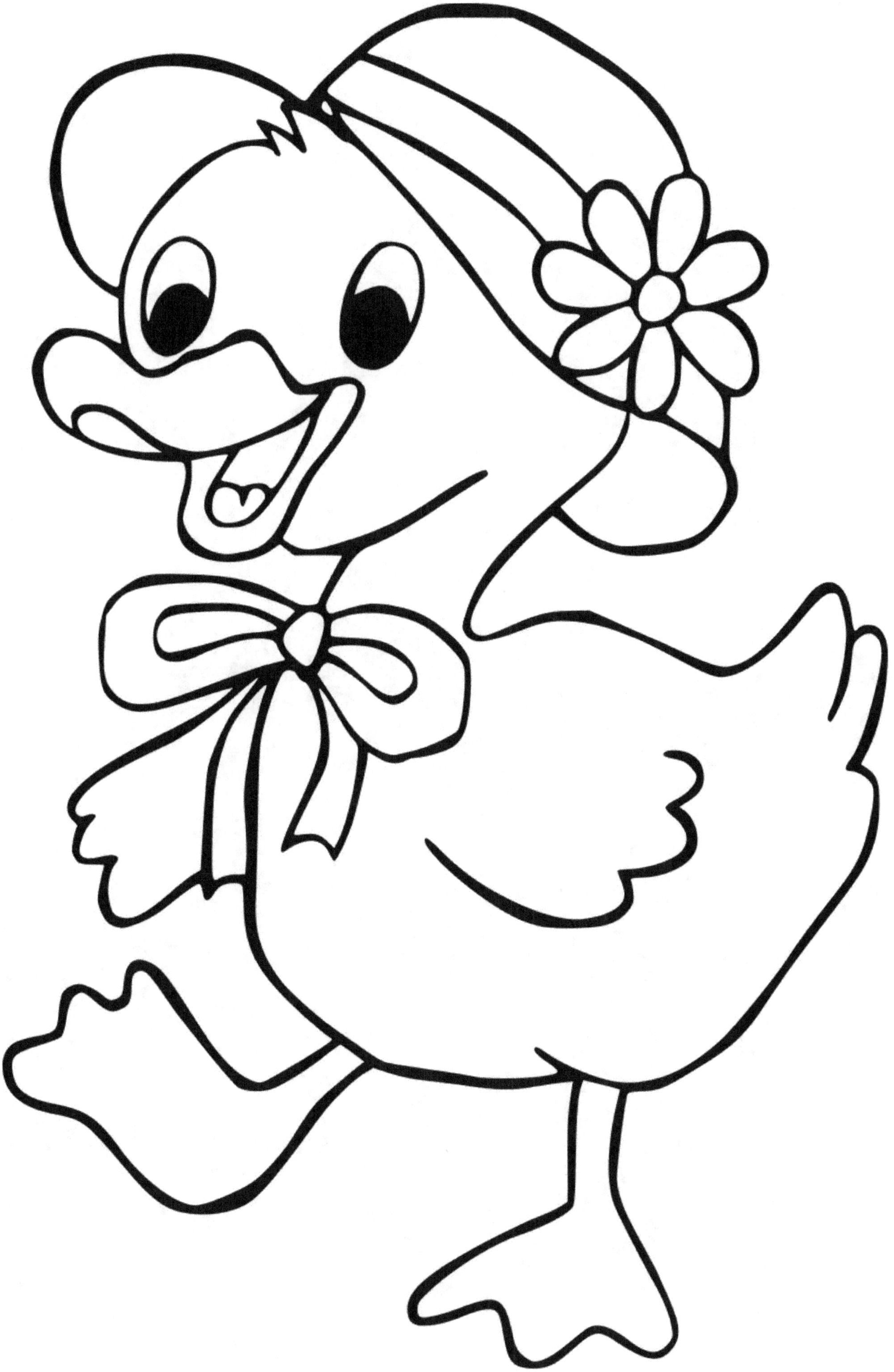

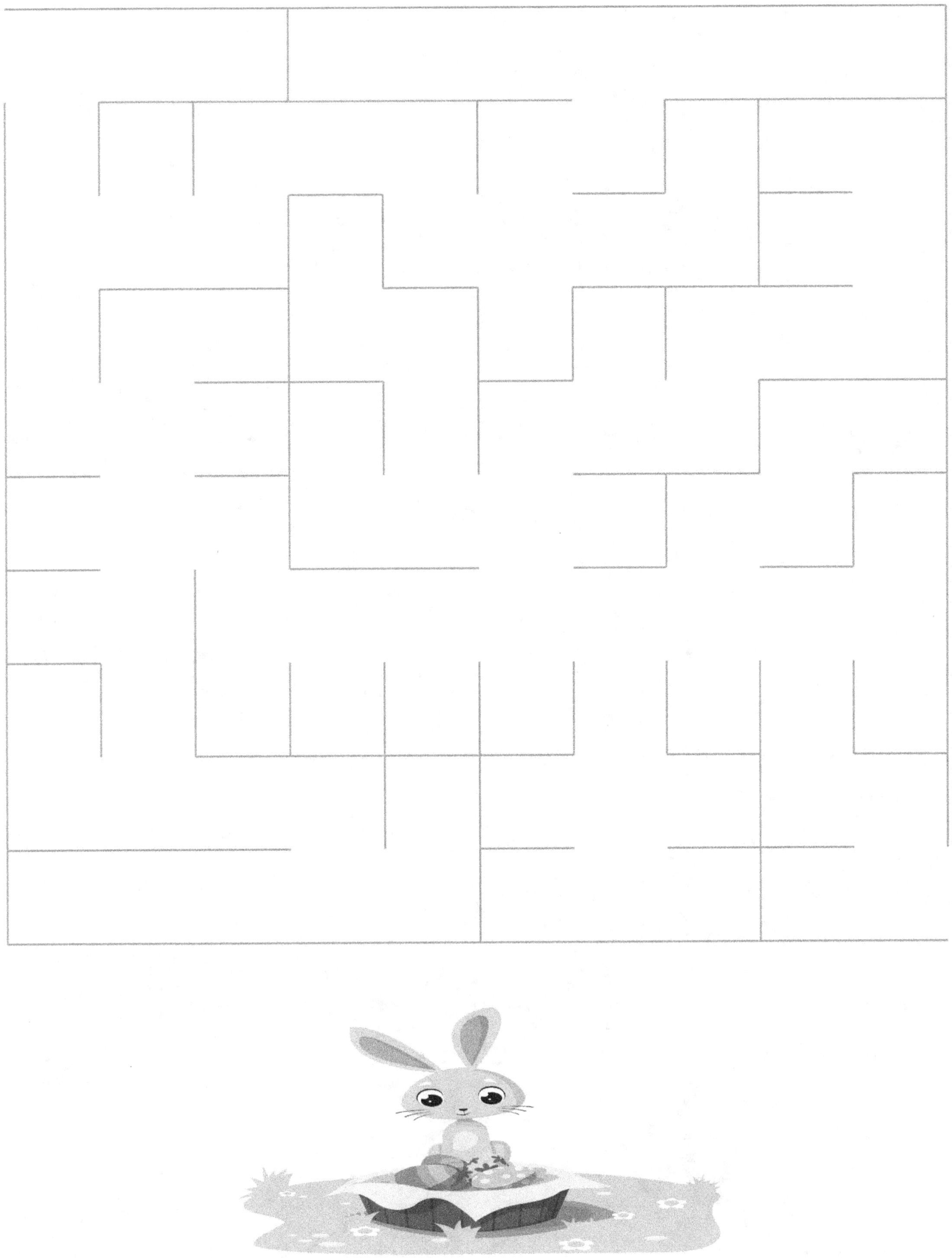

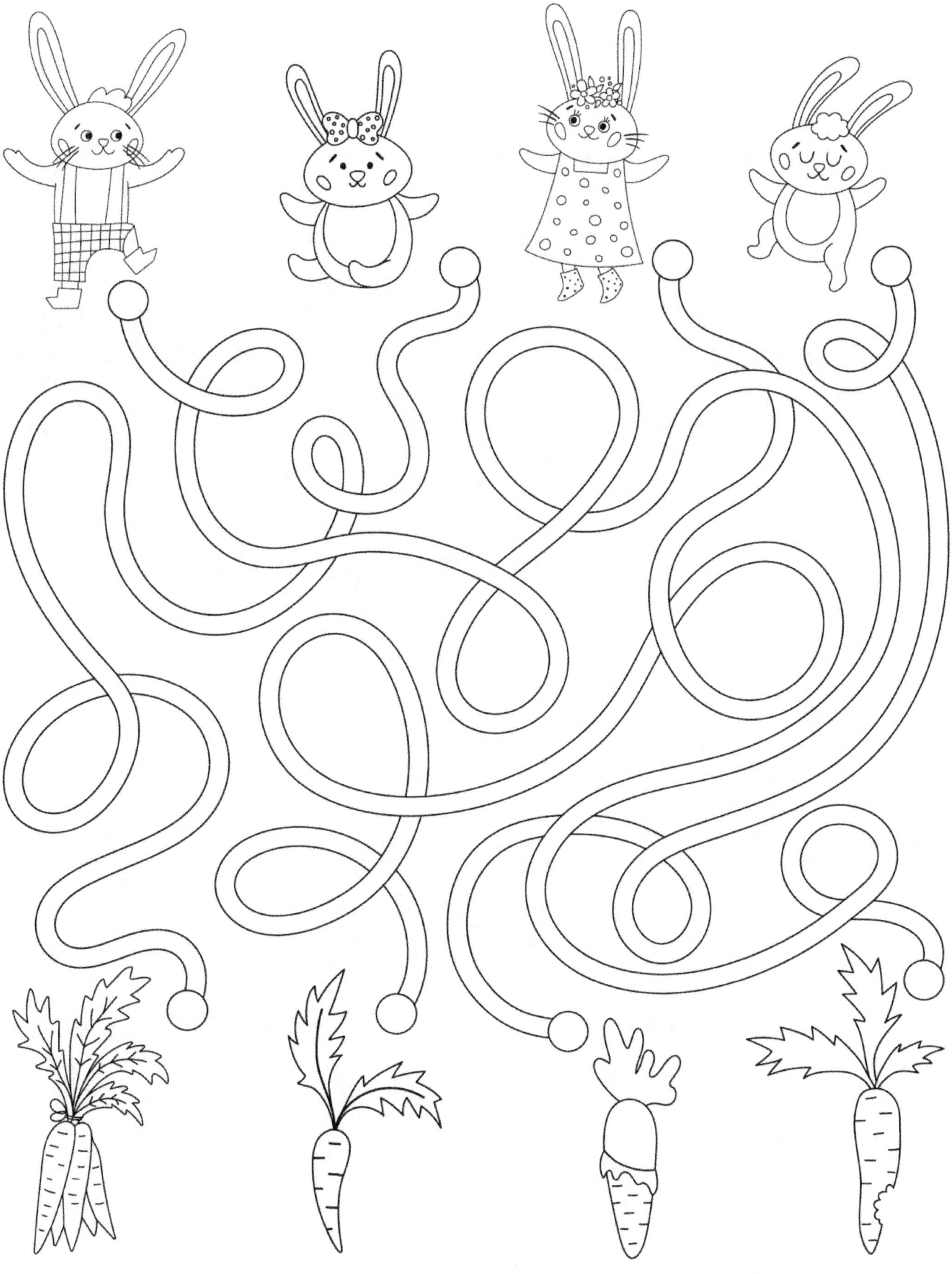

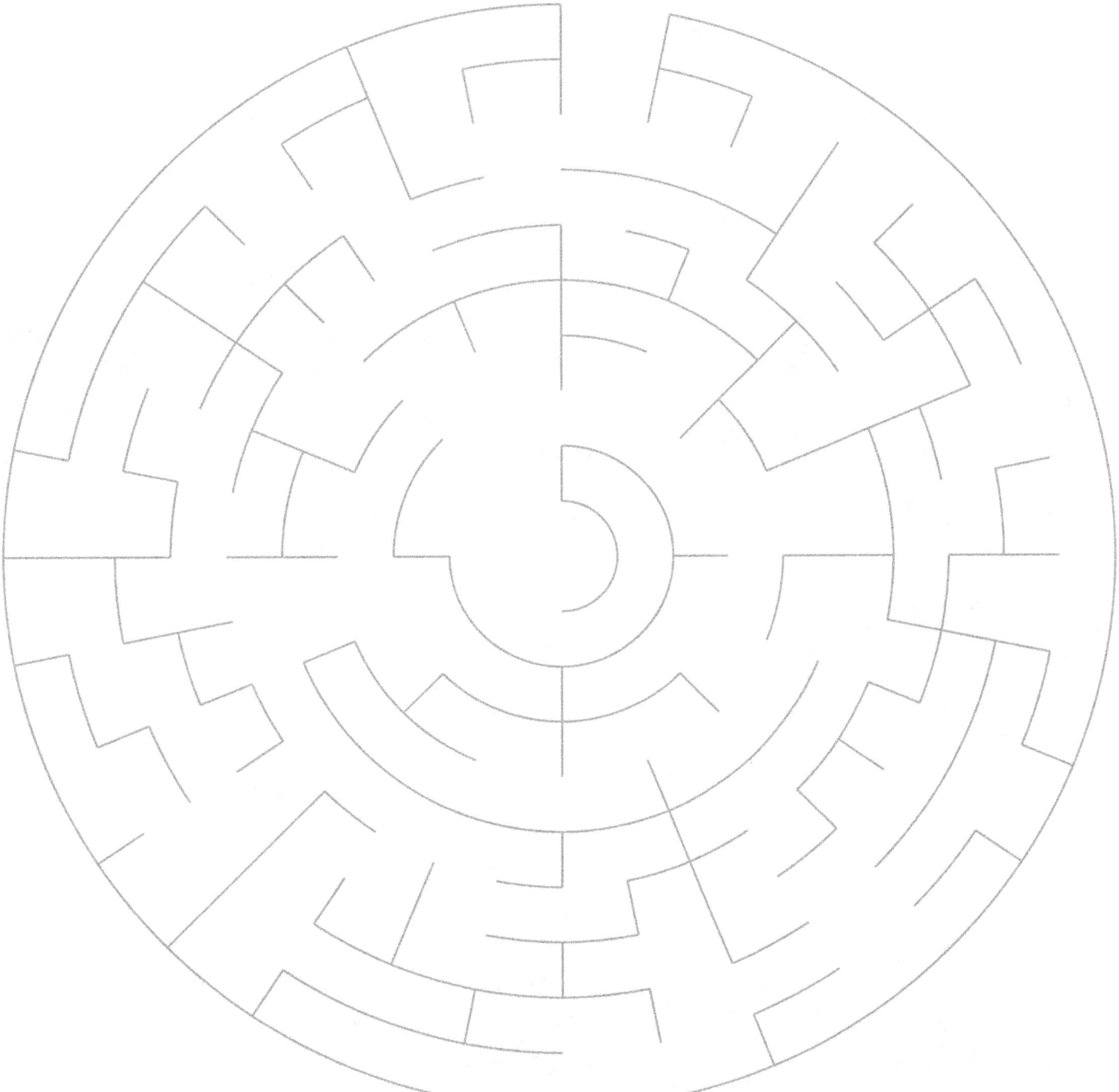

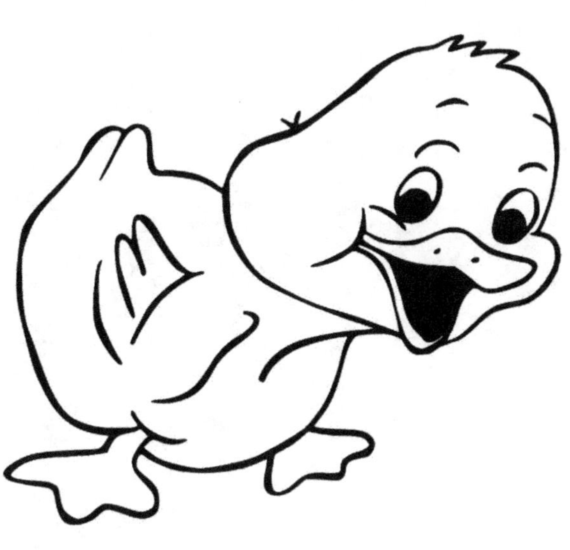

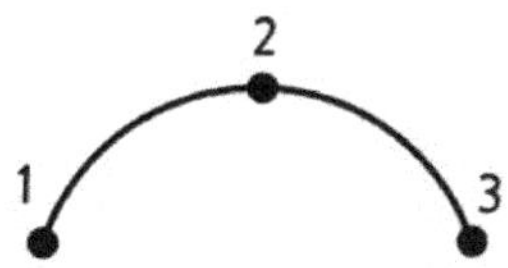


# Connect the Dots

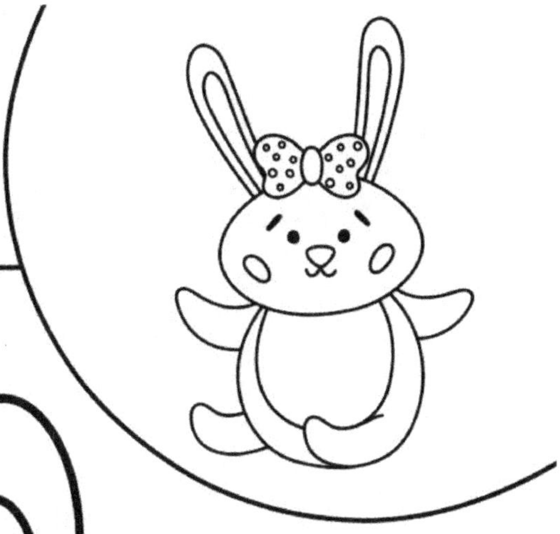

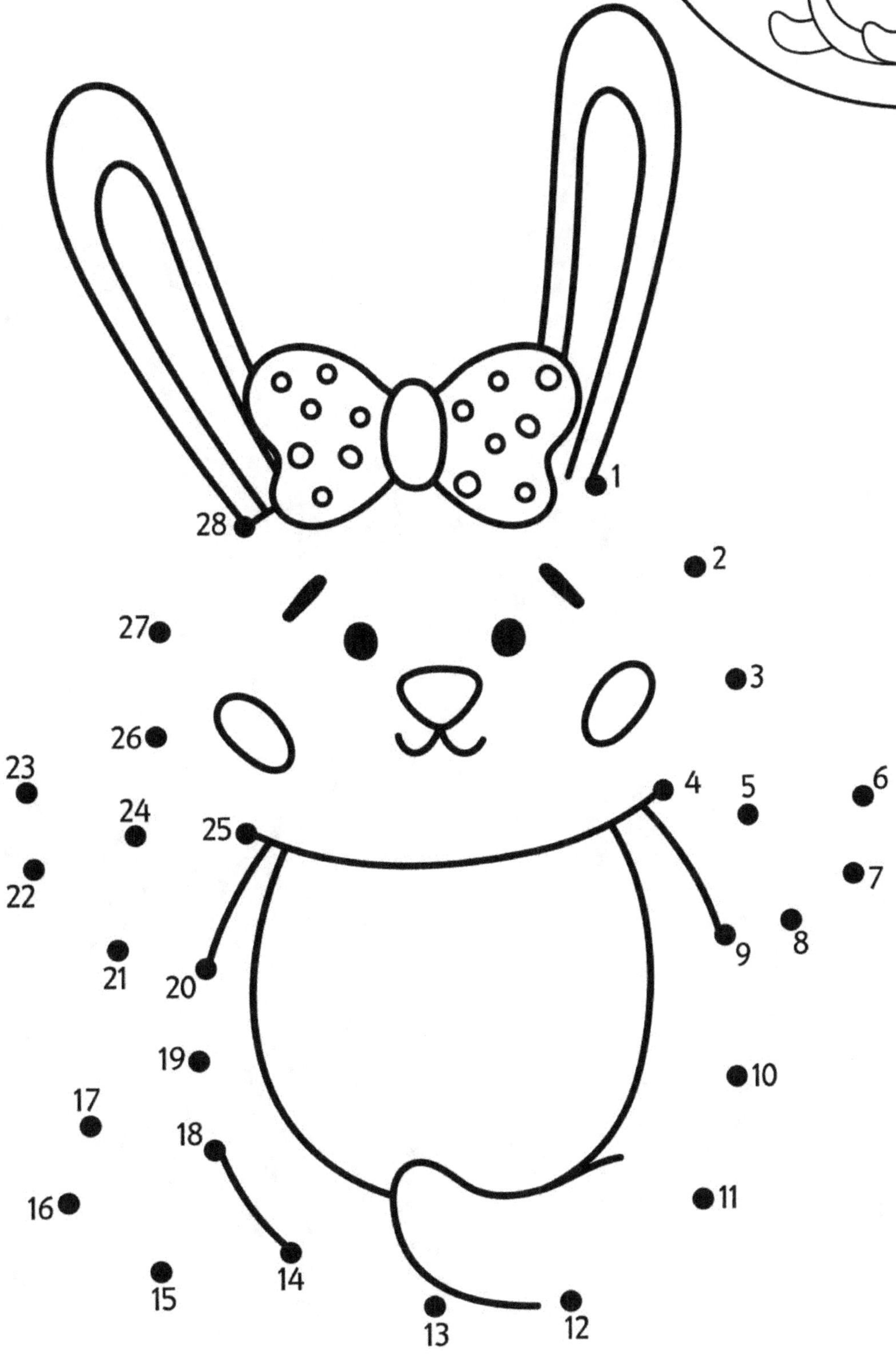

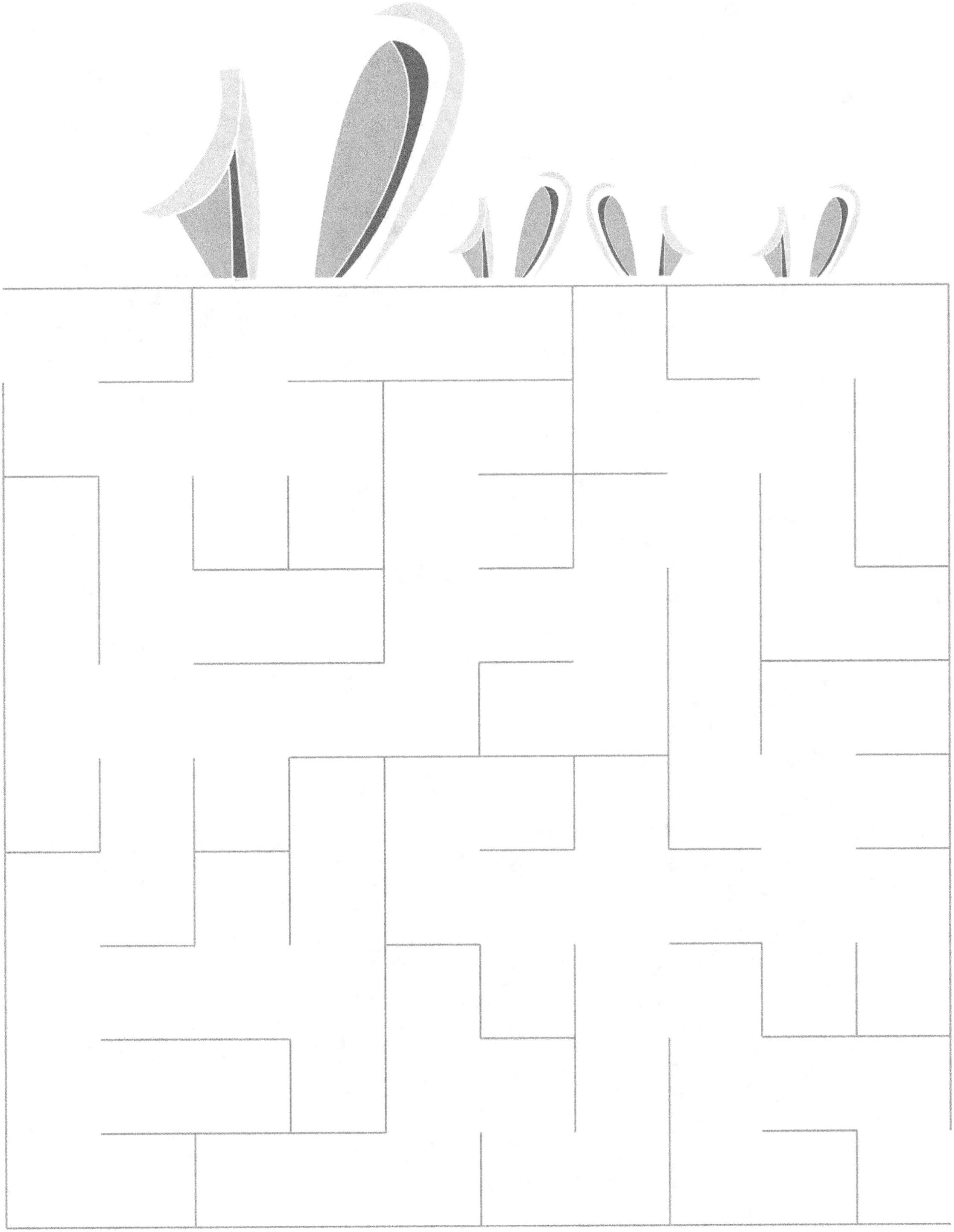

# Let's draw !

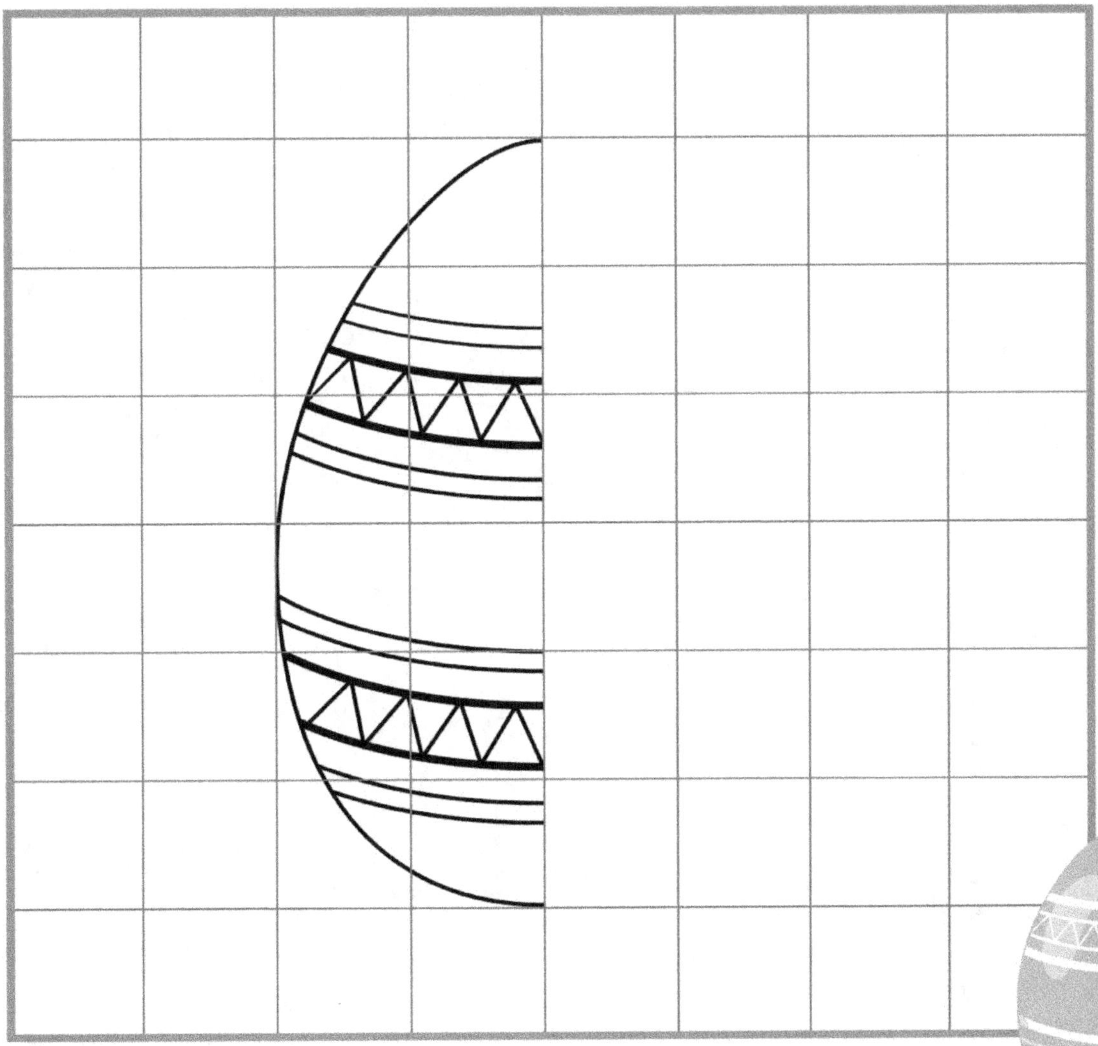

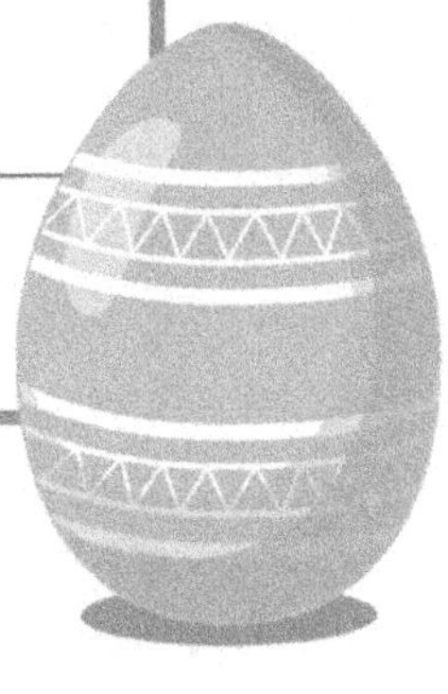

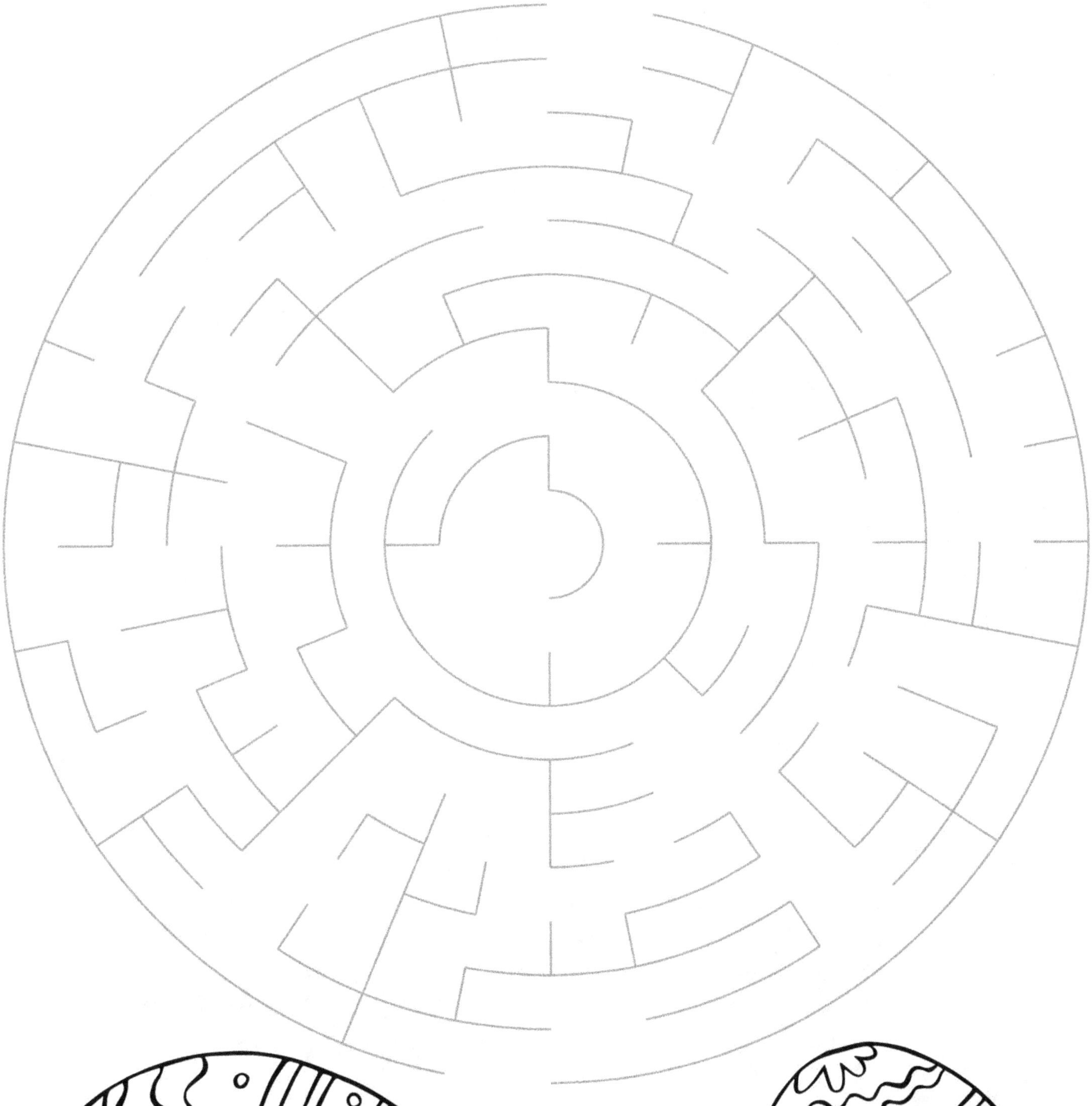

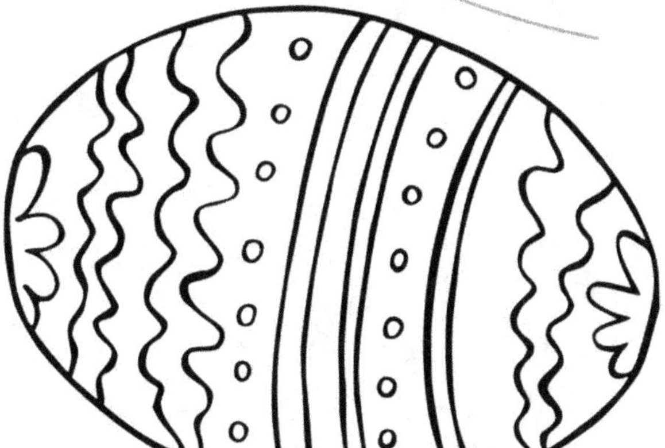

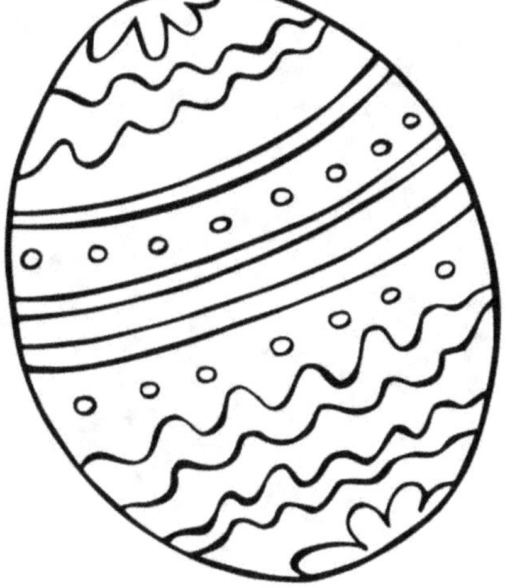

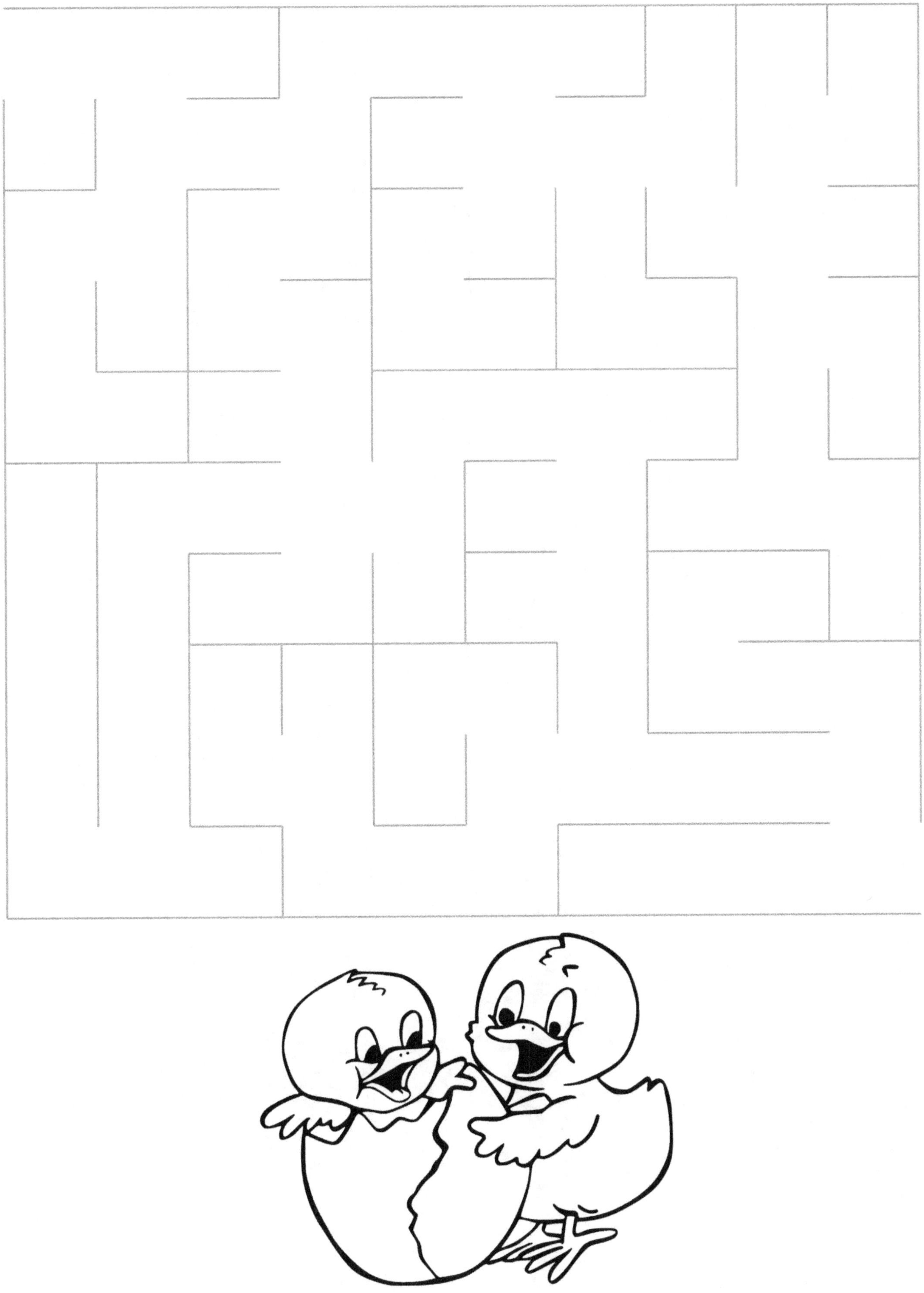

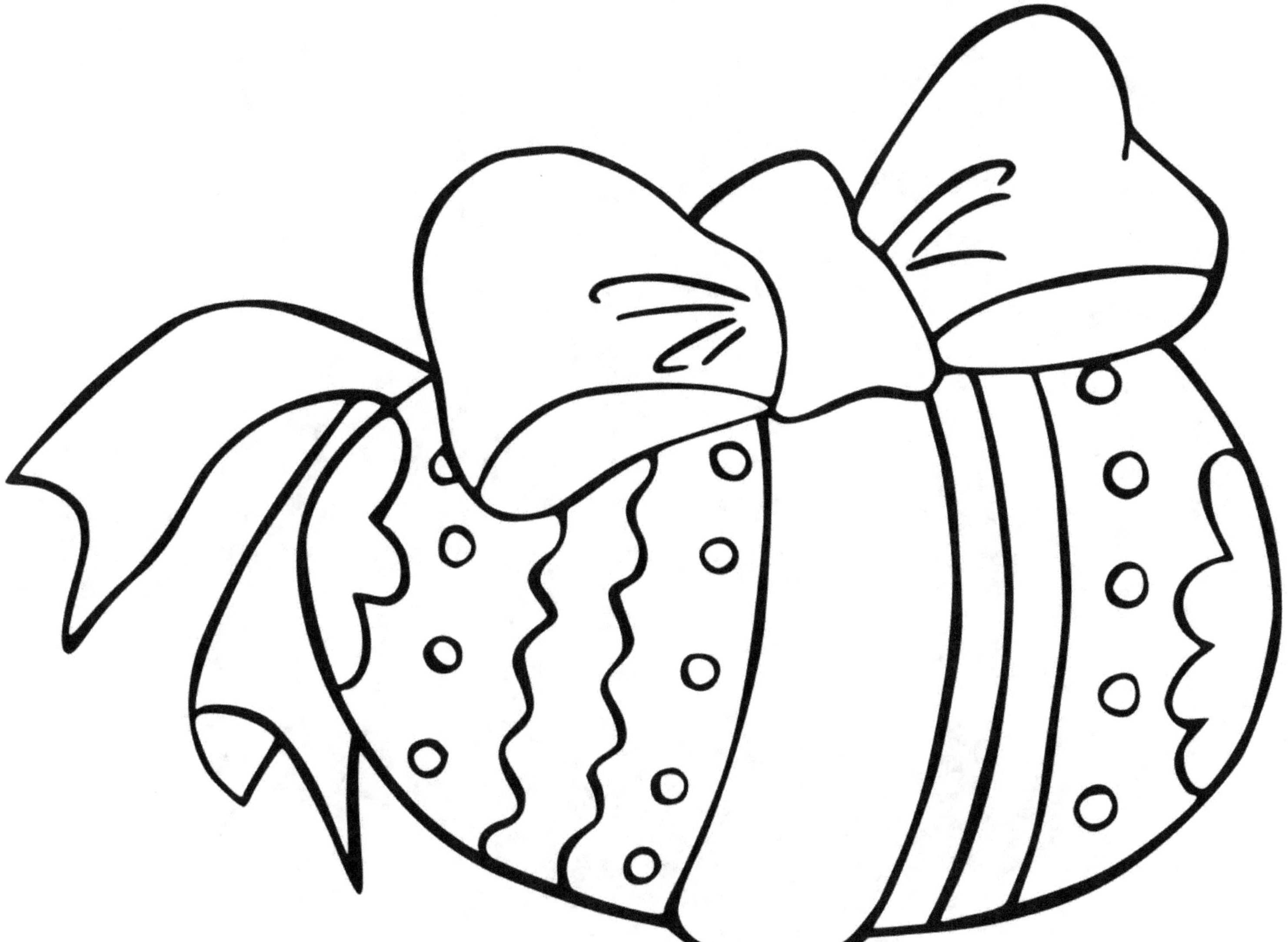

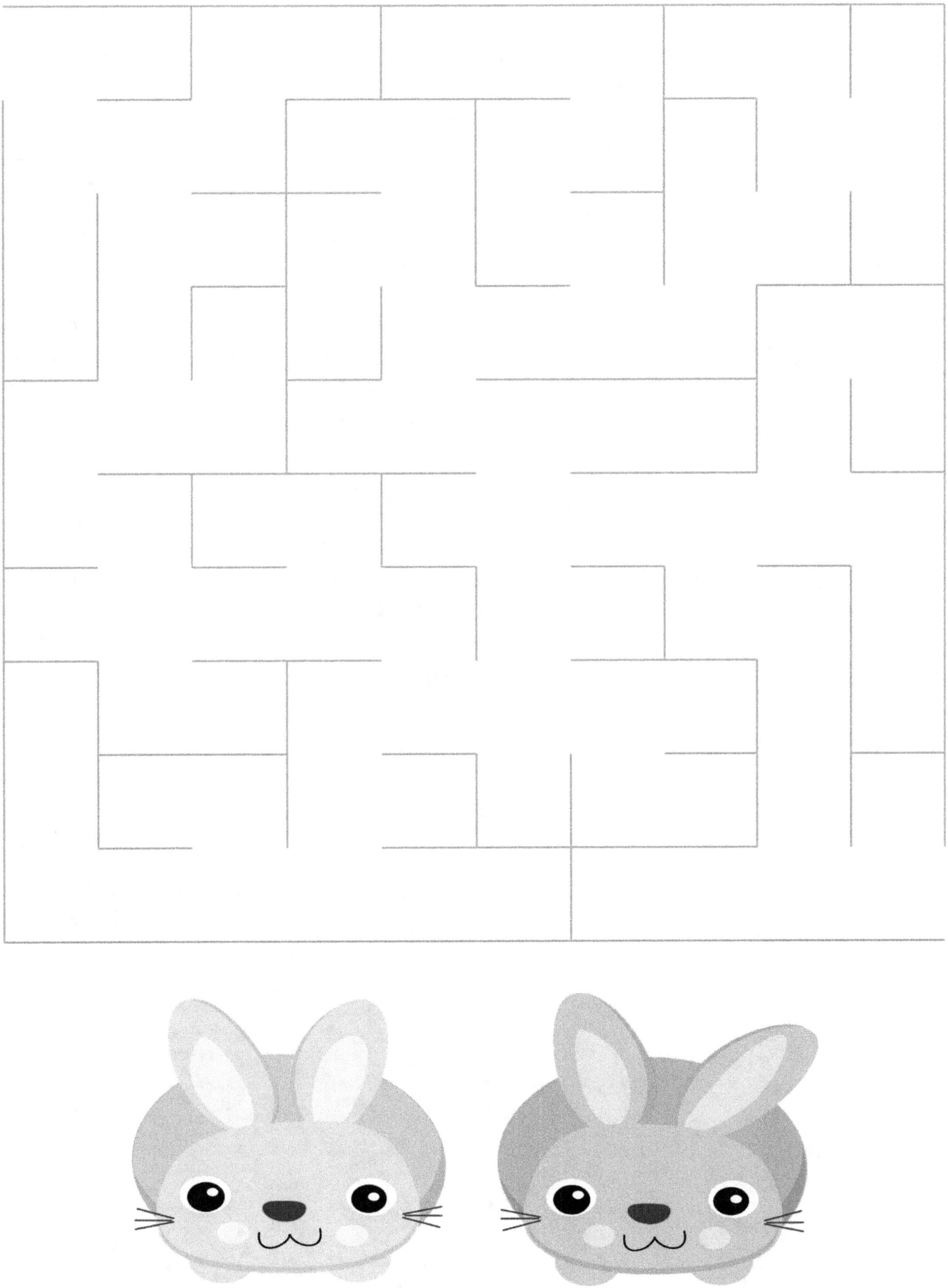

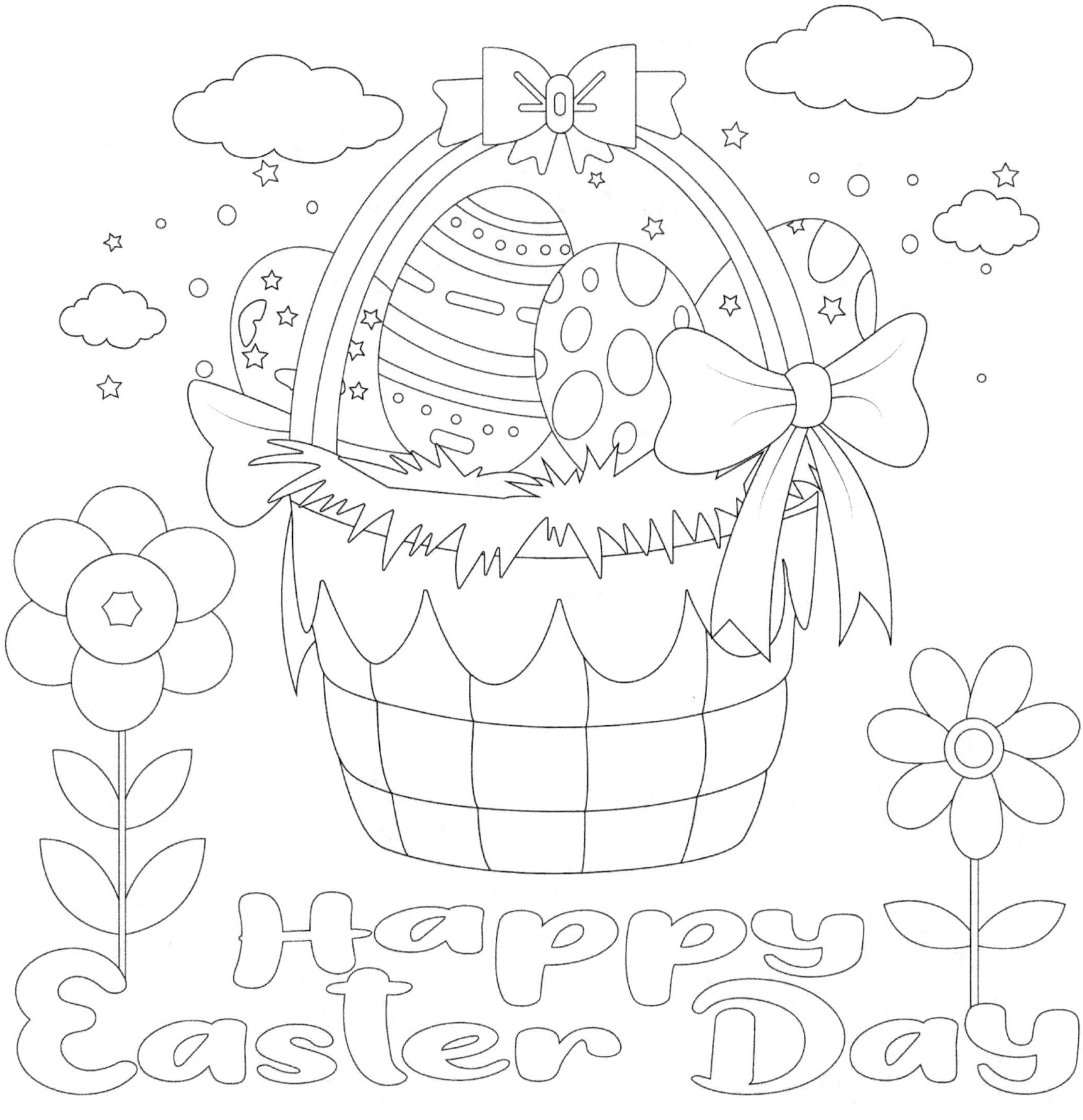
Happy
Easter Day

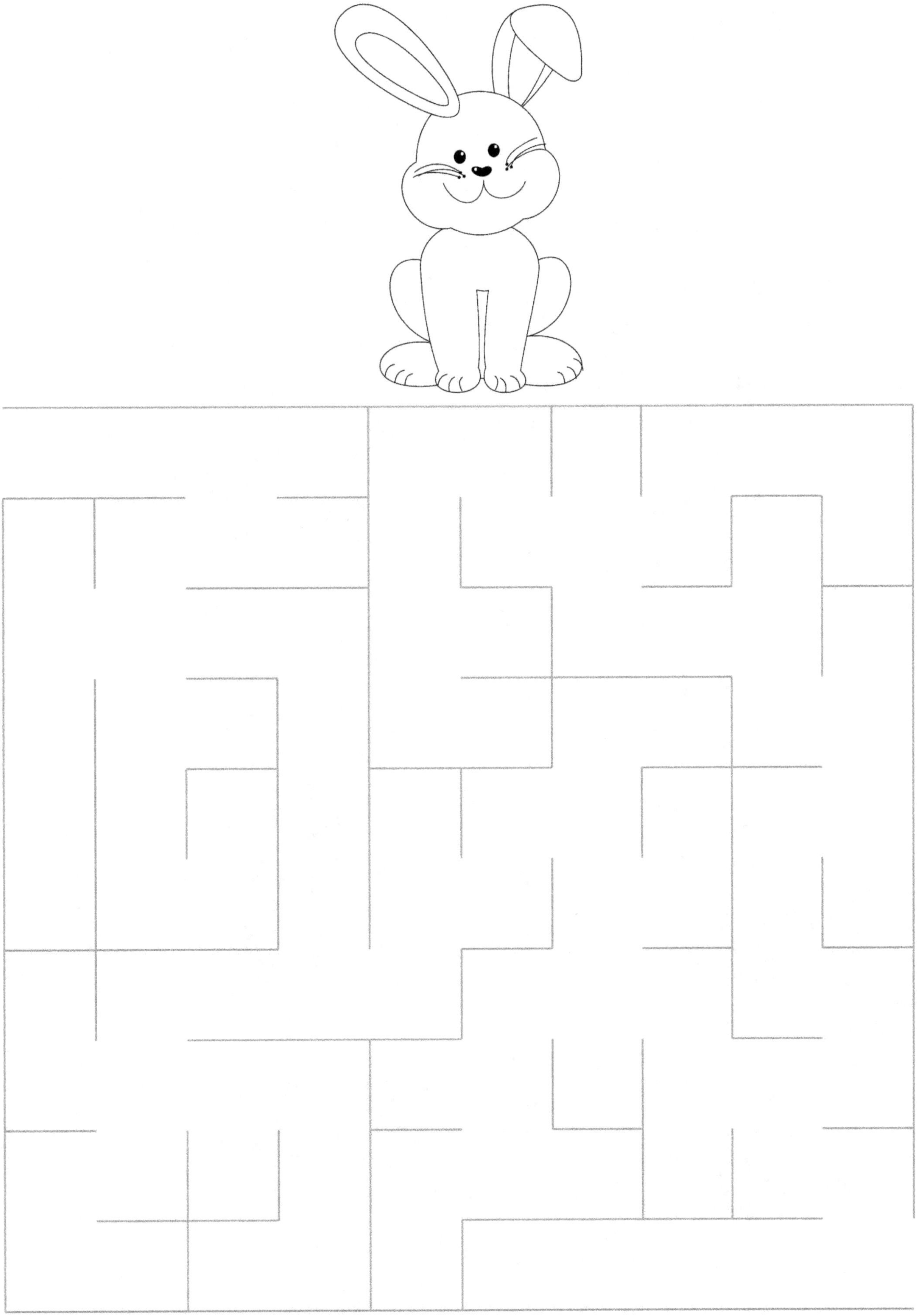

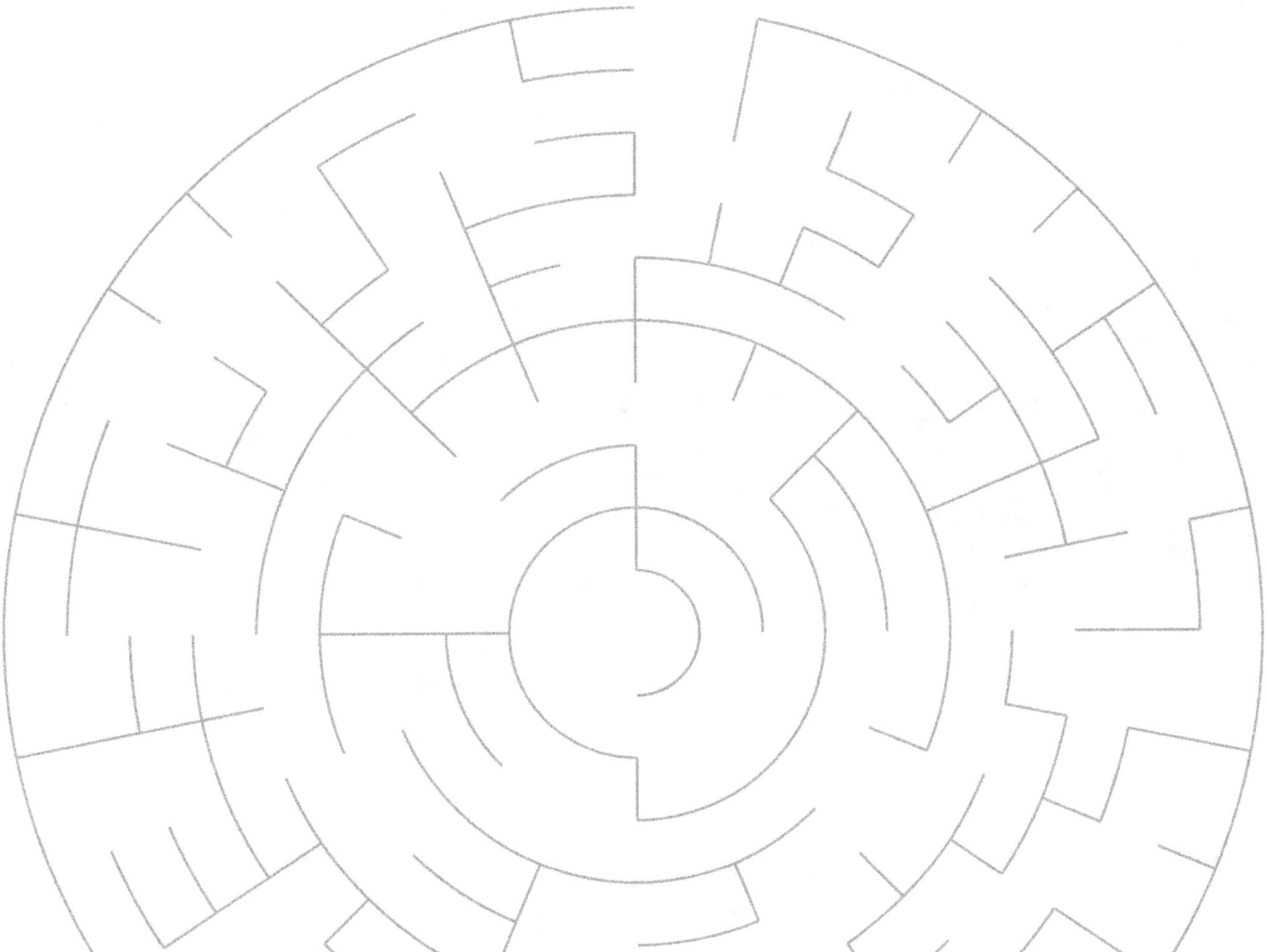

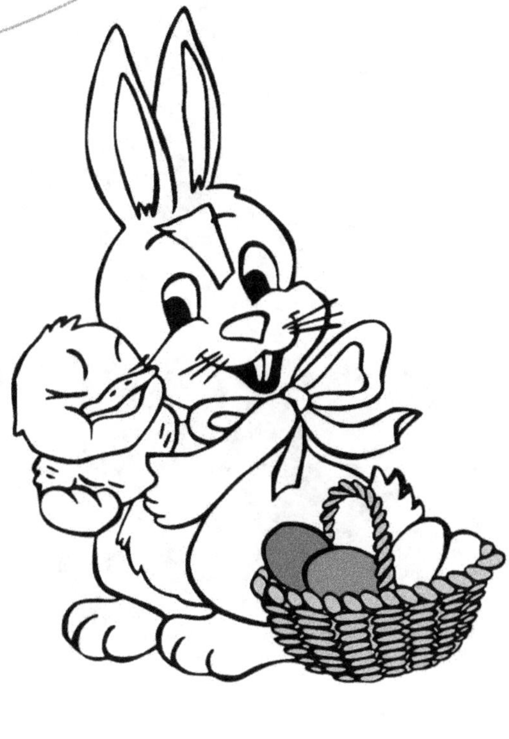

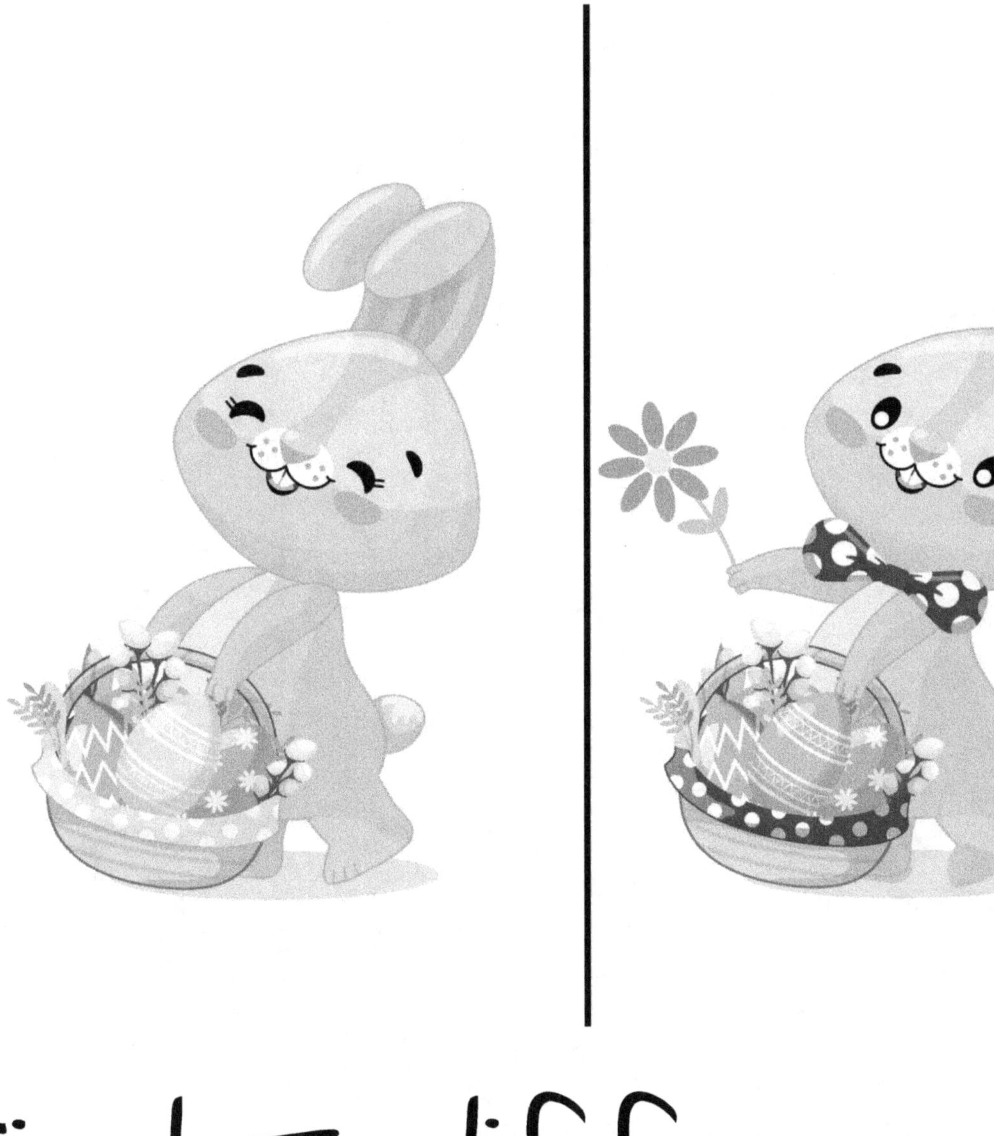

# Find 7 differences

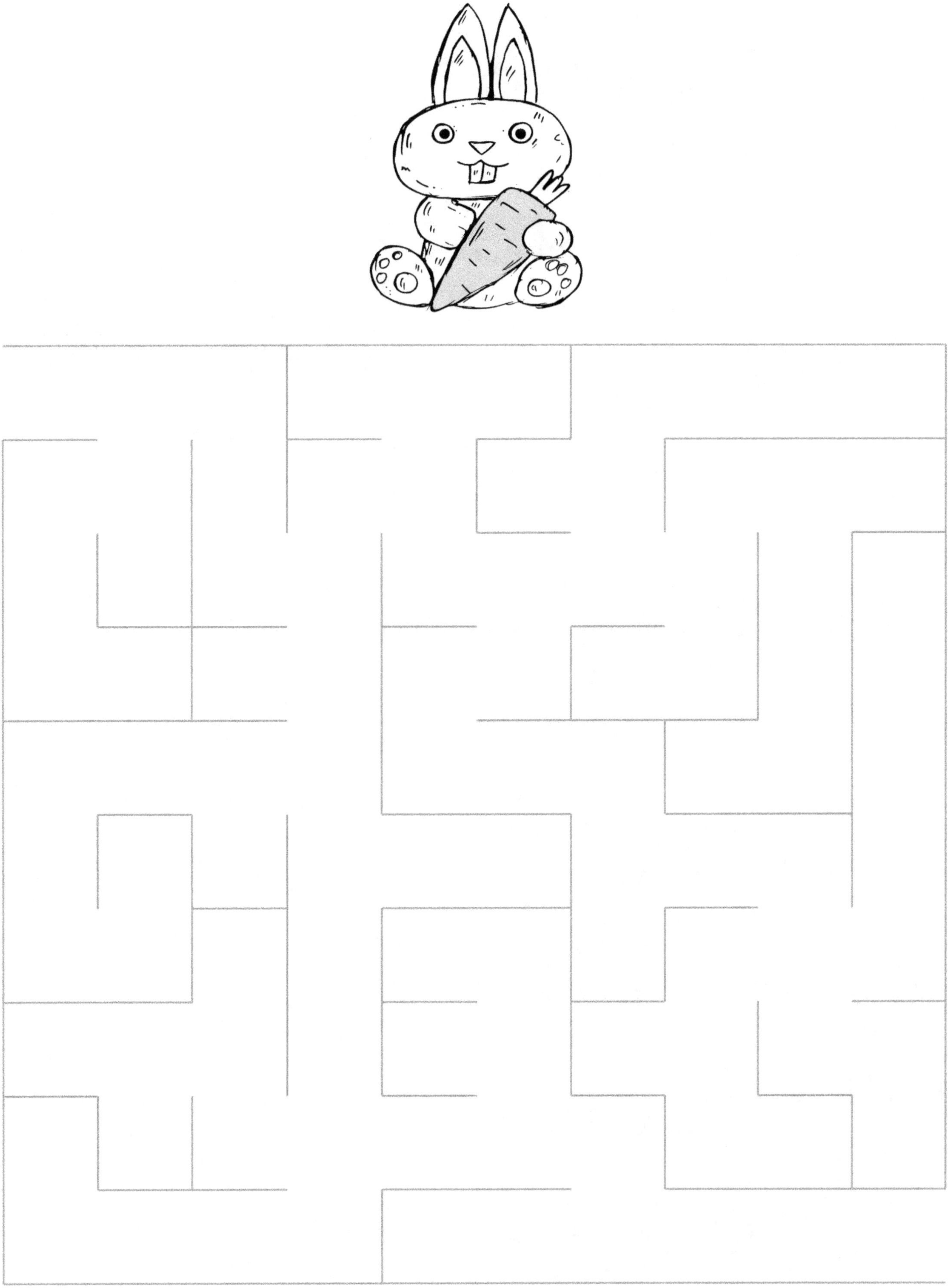

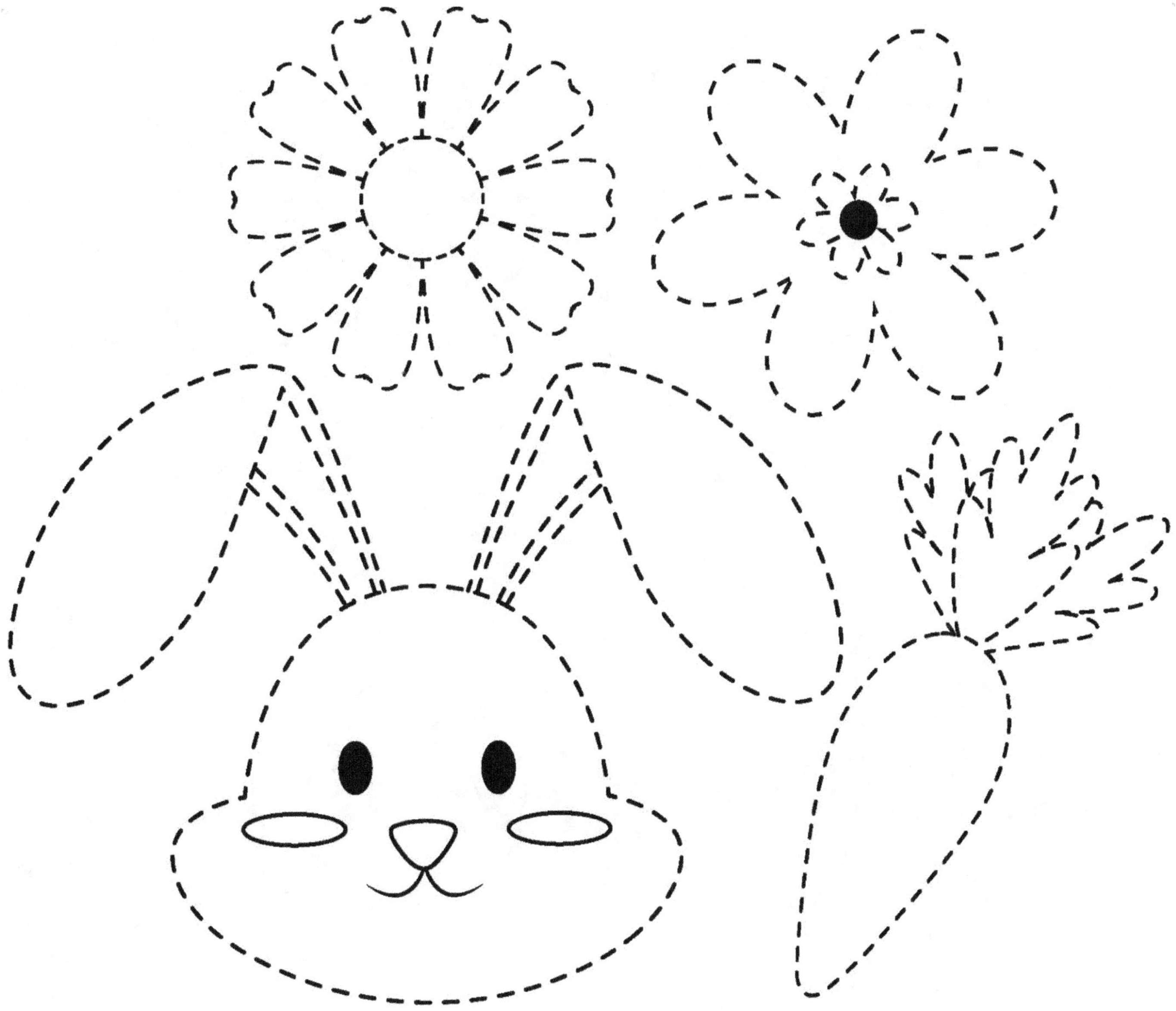

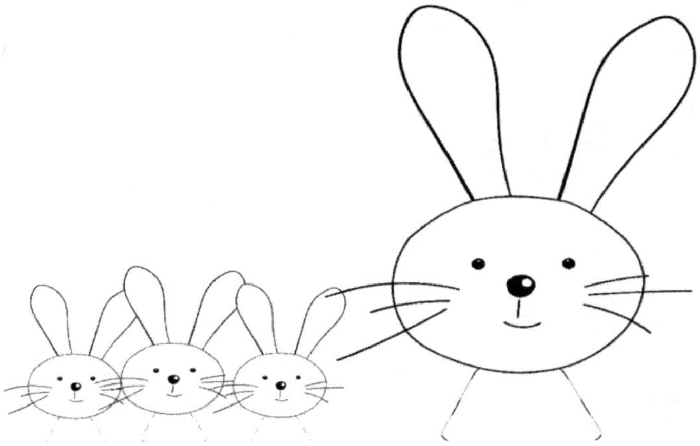
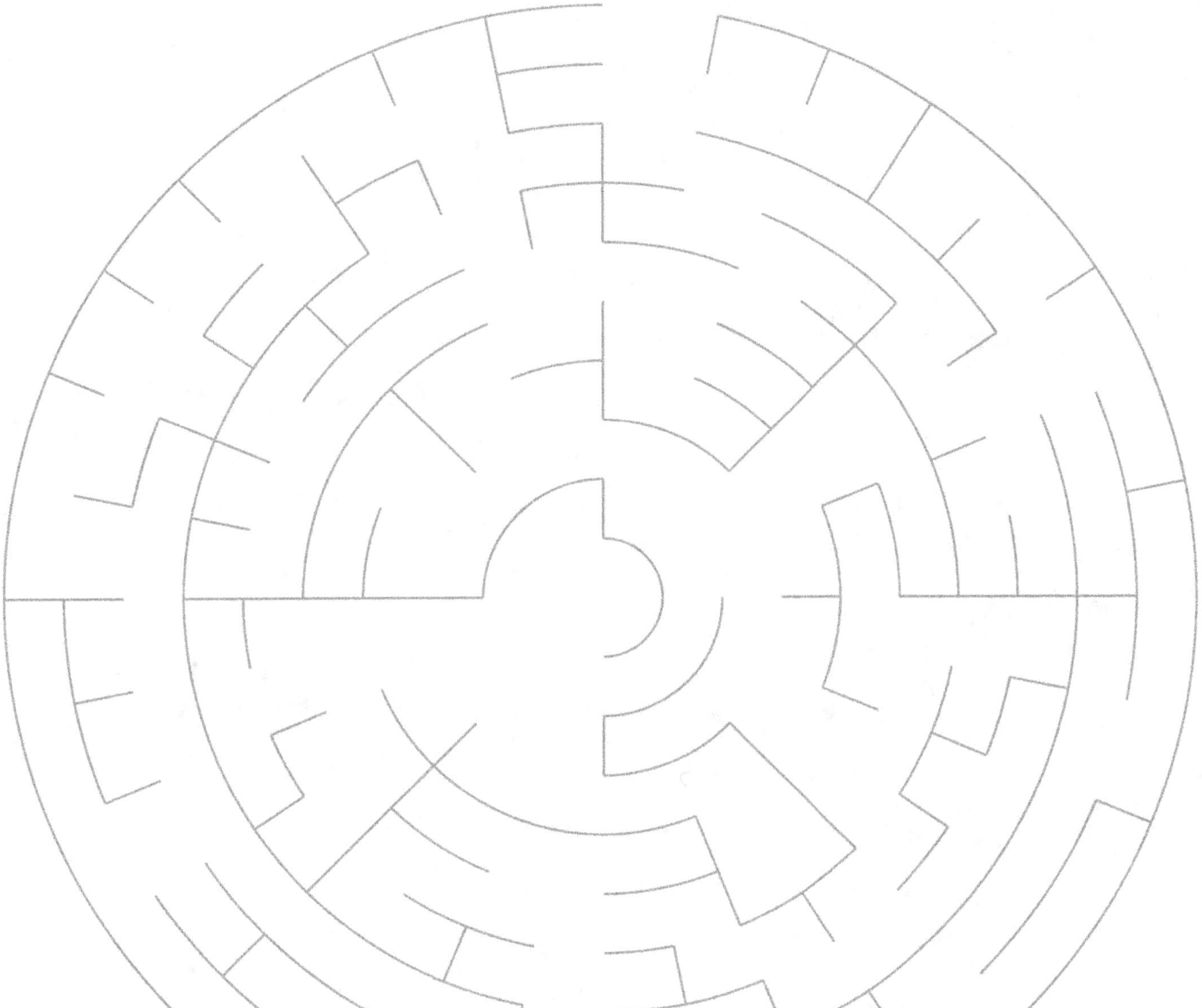

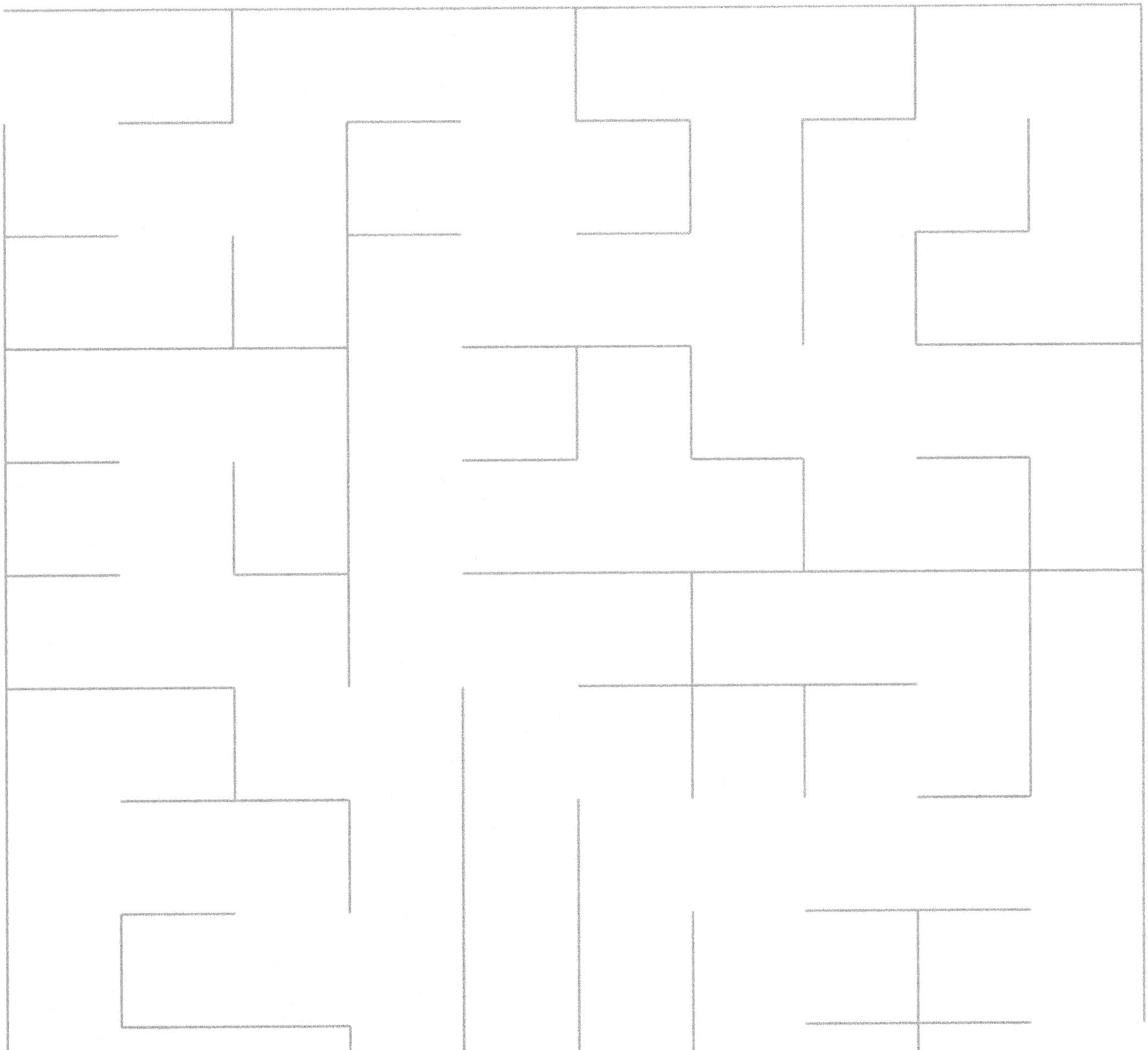

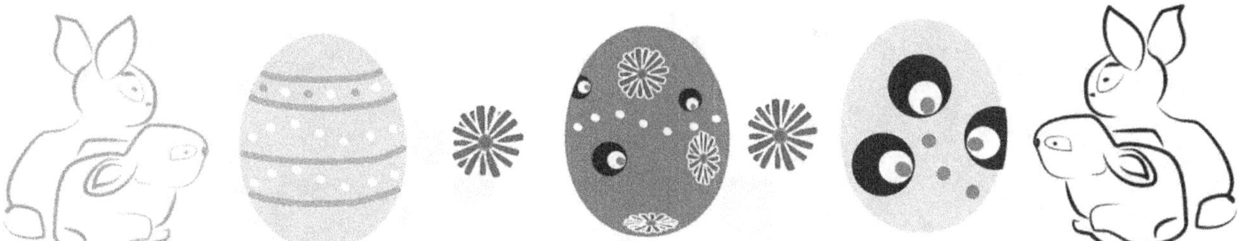

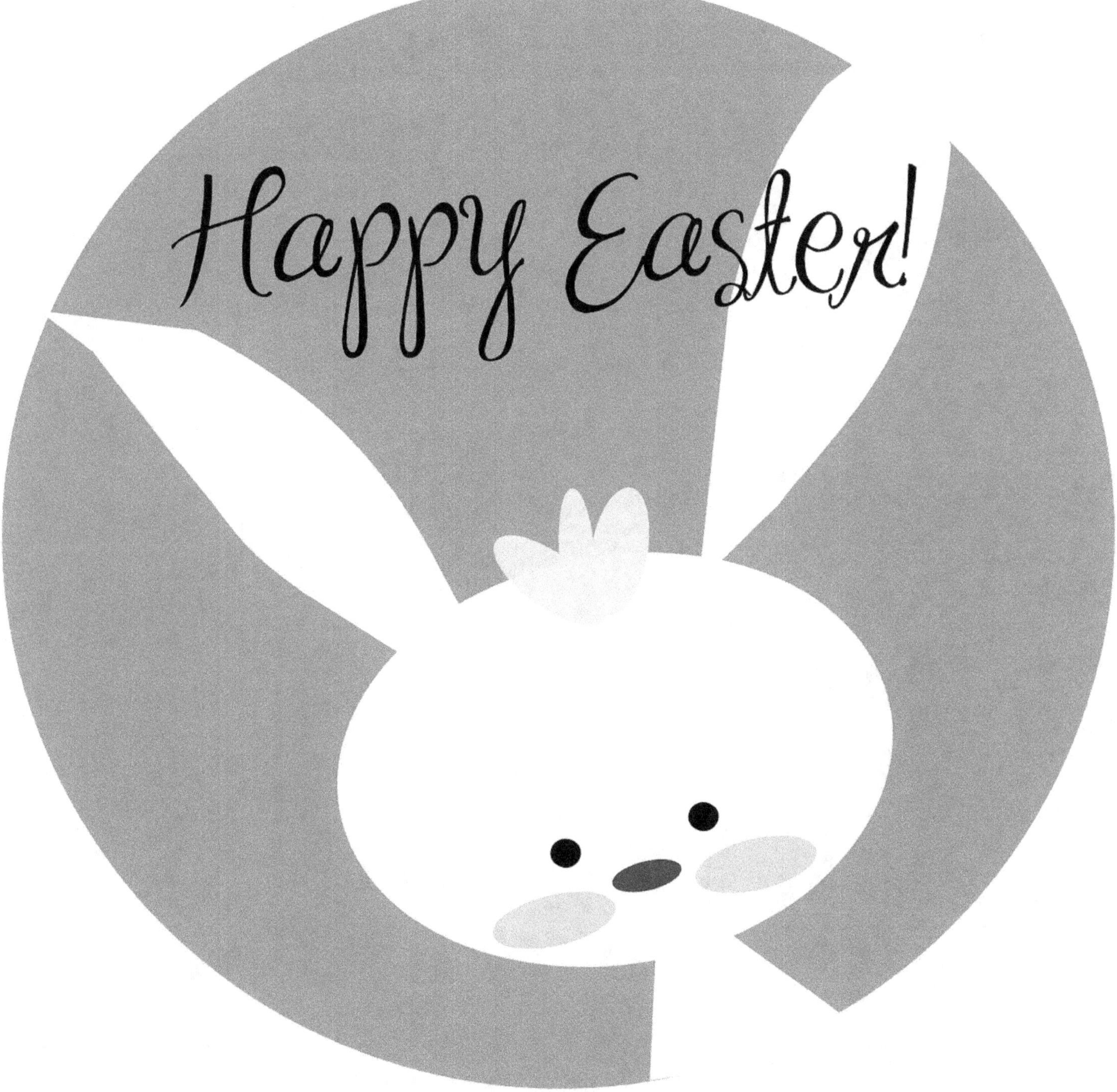
Happy Easter!

www.ingramcontent.com/pod-product-compliance
Lightning Source LLC
Chambersburg PA
CBHW062011220526
45467CB00032BA/2743
*9798378352234*